Skills for OU Study

Develop Effective Study Strategies

The Open University Walton Hall, Milton Keynes MK7 6AA

Edited, designed and typeset by The Open University.

Printed in the United Kingdom by Bell & Bain Ltd., Glasgow

ISBN 978-0-7492-1268-1

1.1

Mixed Sources
Product group from well-managed forests and other controlled sources
www.fsc.org   Cert no. TT-COC-002769
© 1996 Forest Stewardship Council

The paper used in this publication contains pulp sourced from forests independently certified to the Forest Stewardship Council (FSC) principles and criteria. Chain of custody certification allows the pulp from these forests to be tracked to the end use (see www.fsc-uk.org).

Skills for OU Study

Develop Effective Study Strategies

Studying can be more enjoyable if you take time to think about how you learn effectively. This booklet accompanies the Skills for OU Study website http://www.open.ac.uk/skillsforstudy/, which includes advice and activities to help you develop as a learner.

Contents

1 Why think about your learning?

Your capacity to learn can be improved by:

- being motivated
- having a clear purpose
- analysing how you do things
- being willing to try new things
- recognising what works best for you.

If you take some time to think through how you as an individual learn effectively, you'll find that:

- studying will be more enjoyable
- it will be easier to understand course material
- you'll tend to remember course themes, concepts or techniques, which will help when you come to write assignments or prepare for exams.

Finding out about how you learn can help you to develop study techniques that suit your needs and the task at hand. Improving your study strategies will save you time, lighten your workload and help to improve the quality of your work.

Recognise and build on your strengths and make sensible decisions about how to deal with problems.

Spend a bit of time taking stock while you're studying. You'll be able to recognise and build on your strengths and make sensible decisions about how to deal with problems. Learning from feedback on your course assignments, reflecting and being prepared to try new things are important aspects of being an independent and effective learner.

It is also important to keep in mind two things about learning.

- There is no single method of learning that guarantees success. How you learn best depends on many different factors, and you need to find out which approaches to learning and study techniques work well for you – this also depends on the situation or task at hand.
- Although we all differ in the way we learn, there are key approaches and methods that tend to be effective for many of us (e.g. active reading and being creative in taking notes).

 Find out more about active reading and note taking techniques with the Skills for OU Study website at http://www.open.ac.uk/skillsforstudy/

Although there are approaches to learning that seem to work well for a range of study activities, you'll find that particular subjects do require the development of particular learning skills. For example, you can try to learn computer programming by reading about it (there are books on computer languages), but it is easier and more appropriate to learn by actually programming and writing computer programs.

Disciplines or subjects such as history, business studies or biology have particular research traditions, academic practices and conventions. This means that you'll find generic ways of learning and studying that are valuable, but if you're taking a particular programme, or specialising in a subject area you'll become increasingly familiar with the practices of the discipline and the study approaches that are required. For example, psychology students have to become well-versed in research methods that are used in psychology. If a student writes up say, an experimental report for their psychology course, they need to adhere to the guidelines for report writing, which relate to the accepted practices of reporting research studies in the field.

If you move between different subject areas (from say, art history to a science course) then you'll need to recognise that the established practices of the discipline will feel rather unfamiliar. You'll need to give yourself time to develop the particular skills that a new subject requires. For example, in taking science courses you'll need to become familiar with interpreting complex graphs – a skill that is not likely to be needed in arts-based disciplines.

1.1 Learning outcomes

Learning outcomes can help you to be clear about what you'll be learning on a course, and the kinds of skills that you'll develop.

Your course guide or materials include learning outcomes that outline the key intellectual, practical and professional skills you should gain on the course. These skills are usually categorised into four groups.

- Knowledge and understanding. Gaining specific knowledge related to a particular subject (e.g. facts and concepts in scientific areas).

- Cognitive skills. Thinking skills, such as problem solving and analysis.

- Practical and professional skills. Skills related to a vocational area (e.g. web design or lesson planning).

- Key skills. Skills gained as a result of study, such as communication skills and time management.

These can help you to be clear about what you'll be learning on a course, and the kinds of skills that you'll develop.

1.2 Your learning history

There are key factors that are likely to affect you as a learner and your approach to learning and studying. These include:

- your experiences as a learner, both in formal settings (e.g. at school) and informally, through unstructured or unexpected learning experiences (e.g. learning at a museum)
- your motivations (such as the reasons why you are taking a particular course of study)
- your feelings or emotions, which can relate to your previous experiences of learning
- your existing strengths, preferences, habits or skills.

These factors can influence how you experience and engage with your current study, and have implications for the study techniques that you tend to use (which may or may not be effective).

Your experiences as a learner

Think about your experiences of learning. These may be when you were growing up or, more recently, at work. Try to identify:

- an enjoyable and effective learning experience
- an experience that was not enjoyable, or where you perhaps struggled to understand or learn something.

Reflect on *why* the first was more effective, and what the difficulties were with the less positive experience.

It is likely that you'll have some emotional feelings about why you remembered these particular experiences. Emotions and feelings are often part of our learning, and recognising this – and resolving any tensions in our feelings about learning – is an important part of developing as a learner.

By looking at your experiences you can:

- begin to address how you can now take control of your learning
- try effective techniques that will see you through your studies.

Related online resources

Learning with the OU at http://www.open.ac.uk/learning brings together resources that will help you develop a variety of qualities and skills, which will be invaluable for OU study, work and other areas of your life.

Here, you can also access an online eportfolio tool to keep track of your learning, maintain personal development planning records, and develop CVs.

2 Active learning

What do we mean by active learning? In active learning you *engage* with the subject matter or topic areas, and think through the course themes, methods, ideas and concepts. It is sometimes too easy to simply get out your materials and read, rather than working out ways to understand the course material. Take an active approach by:

- building on your existing knowledge

- continually asking questions about the topics to be learned

- doing things, such as taking notes that help make the topic meaningful to you.

Learning is not a straightforward linear process. It can be useful to think of learning as an ongoing process in which you advance your understanding. Aspects of your learning can be viewed as a learning spiral (see Figure 1). For example, as you 'move around' the spiral sometimes you realise that the ideas you once had difficulty grasping are now more clear to you, and you want to move on to take in new ideas and think them through.

To be successful in your studies, you also need to feel motivated and want to learn. Ideally, you are interested in the course and have identified your own goals relating to your studies. Be mindful of your:

- short-term goals that can vary (e.g. getting to grips with a difficult concept, completing an assignment)

- long-term goals, which might include those relating to your career development, such as passing a course, or obtaining a qualification.

This approach will help when you need to get going with a particular study task, and when you need to find ways to manage your time and prioritise.

Sometimes study strategies or skills are presented as if they'll work for most, if not all students. In reality you'll find that you'll have preferences, styles or habits that work for you. It is worth bearing in mind that different strategies are useful in different contexts and with particular study tasks and activities. You need to recognise what works for you generally, and which strategies are valuable for more specific activities.

Figure 1   The Learning spiral

Source: Northedge, A. and Lane, A. (1997) 'What is learning?' In Northedge, A., Thomas, J., Lane, A. and Peasgood, A., The Sciences Good Study Guide, Milton Keynes, Open University, pp. 20-2.

> ❛ I learn mostly by listening. I thought, I'm going to get myself a digital voice recorder and tape myself. So now that's exactly what I do. I tape myself reading passages in my book, or whatever, and I record pertinent points on my digital recorder. Then I can play them back on my iPod. It's really good for on the move as well as when I'm at home. ❜

There are theories that suggest that we tend to adopt particular approaches to study or learning styles. You may find that you prefer to learn from a 'hands-on' approach by, for example, visiting a museum to help you with a topic in science. Some students find that they are good at remembering information visually and benefit from using mind maps or learning posters that they can pin on the wall. Other students find it valuable to listen to a recording from their course materials as it's easier for them to process information in this way.

It can, therefore, be useful to recognise your preferred style of learning and then re-think how you might use study techniques effectively.

2.1 The importance of feedback

Learning from feedback is an important activity in developing as a learner. Continuous assessment in the OU is not just a mechanism for judging your performance as a student, it is also meant to be part of the process of learning – but you do need to engage with this process.

A great deal of learning takes place through completing course activities and assignments, and getting feedback on them. For example, during the course you may use online discussion forums for a course activity where you work with other students. This provides an opportunity to get feedback on your ideas or understanding of a topic.

Look at feedback carefully as there may be advice that you could act on and incorporate into future assignments.

You'll receive feedback on your assignments and it's important to look at it carefully each time as there may be advice that you could act on and incorporate into future assignments, which could enhance your grades. Sometimes it helps to wait a few days to read the feedback again, as you may find that you can then be more objective.

- Are the comments expected?
- Do you agree with the comments? If not, in what ways do you disagree?
- What steps can you take to address the issues raised in the comments?
- What specific skills do you think you need to improve?

Ask your tutor or study adviser if you have any queries about anything in the feedback. You can also ask them for advice on improving your study skills.

3 Learning skills

Learning skills are also often called study skills or key skills. These key skills, which are needed for study and can be gained as a result of study, are included in the learning outcomes for your course. Examples of these skills include:

- organisational skills (e.g. planning and scheduling how to complete an assignment)

- communication skills (e.g. reading and understanding different sources, and writing in a style that is appropriate to the task)

- numeracy skills (e.g. constructing graphs and applying statistical techniques).

Understanding which skills are needed for a particular task and how effective you are at using them is important. But learning skills are not acquired in a vacuum – you have to be studying something in order to practise or develop them. If you have studied two or more OU courses on different subjects, you may have found that the skills you developed and used in one course did not easily transfer to the other course.

Being aware of what you're good at and where you need to develop your skills can be the first step to boosting your confidence, enabling you to plan to improve your performance as a student. We all have skills that we've used successfully in different areas of our lives, and you can harness these and use them effectively in your studies. If you find there is a specific skill that you need to develop – such as understanding graphs or making notes as you read – then make a decision to improve that skill and set aside the time to do so.

We all have skills that we've used successfully in different areas of our lives, and you can harness these and use them effectively in your studies.

It is possible to become stuck in a study routine that is not actually very effective for the task in hand. Thinking about your own skills and being aware of those you tend to use may help you to:

- see how you might make changes

- develop new ways of working

- become more aware of the different techniques you could devise.

Go to the Skills for OU Study website at http://www.open.ac.uk/skillsforstudy/ to find out how you can identify and improve your skills.

4 Being reflective

Reflection has an important role to play in learning and self-development. There are some key elements of reflection, and you'll need to develop your own preferred ways. Reflection could be described as:

- thinking with a purpose

- being critical, but not negative

- analysing how effective your learning is

- questioning and probing

- making judgements and drawing conclusions.

There are different types of reflection. For example, question-based reflection can be used in a structured way on a course to guide you through the reflective process. Here you engage in reflection by answering a series of questions, which are used as prompts. In contrast, open reflection is relatively unstructured, and techniques such as free writing and mind mapping can be used to generate ideas (Cottrell, 2003).

Get used to reviewing and reflecting on your experiences as part of your everyday learning.

Get used to reviewing and reflecting on your experiences as part of your everyday learning. In this way, each experience - whether positive or negative - will contribute to your development and personal growth. An experience that is repeated without reflection is just a repetition, which does not help you to learn.

- See reflection as complementary to your study.

- Use it to clarify your thoughts and focus on your development.

- Record your thoughts on any difficulties or challenges you are facing.

- Think about any strategies that might help you deal with difficult tasks or assignments.

- Use it to help you think about how the course topics relate to other areas of your experience.

4.1 Tools for reflection

The areas you focus on for reflection differ from person to person, as can the tools you use to record your reflections. You may need to try a few different types to find the one that is most beneficial, and your method of recording reflection may change as time goes by (see Figure 2 and Figure 3). Tools for reflection include:

- learning journals or diaries

- structured forms

- mind maps

- recording yourself on audio.

Learning with the OU

Go to Learning with the OU at http://www.open.ac.uk/learning to access an online eportfolio tool that you can use for your development. You can use it:

- as a reflective tool

- to keep track of your learning

- to maintain personal development planning records.

The use of a reflective learning journal is a common and valuable approach, and you can adopt a structure for each journal entry, which could include the setting and date, what you did, and key critical notes on your reflections about the activity and what you think you learned. It is worth experimenting with different tools that have different structures.

- Some could be ready-made, such as a diary with 'a day to a page'.

- Use your own creation – a note book in which you've stuck your study timetable at the front, and your favourite postcards here and there to inspire you.

> ‘ I've come a long way since doing my first TMA – I suppose I'm starting to develop some reflective skills in that I'm looking back at how my study sessions have gone and having a go at identifying the strategies that work well for me. ’

Date	25th April
Description of event	Tutorial
What did I learn?	Clarified block 3 themes and linked them to what I need to know for the exam.
Short term implications	Useful for the TMA in 3 weeks.
Long term implications	Remember to come back to the themes when I'm revising.
Feedback from others	I found that other students were also confused about the meaning of section 2 – some of us are going to discuss it a bit more on the forum.
What will I do differently?	Get in contact more with other students – it helps to know that others get confused by things on the course too, and talking about it seems to help. I'll make more use of the forums.
Notes	I've still got a query about the TMA question – must ask my tutor.

Figure 2   Structured reflection example

25/4
Went to the tutorial today – it was good to see some of the other students again.
It was also useful because I'm now clearer about the block 3 themes, which should help when I prepare for the exam.

I'm now thinking about the TMA which is due in a few weeks – I'll talk to the tutor about the question.

Talking with the other students today made me realise that it's not just me that gets confused by some of the sections – I'll try and use the forums more often so I can keep in touch with other students and discuss bits of the course.

Figure 3   Example entry from a learning journal

Keeping a reflective learning journal

Here are some tips for keeping a learning journal or diary.

- Write regularly, but remember that entries can be short.

- Focus on a specific issue or problem for an individual entry – think about how you could address or resolve the issue, or what you'd like to improve.

- Use questions or prompts – these can help you focus on the task.

- Avoid descriptive writing – instead, be critical and analytical in your approach. You need to question, disagree, argue and evaluate.

- Use creative note taking techniques, such as mind mapping, or draw diagrams, sketches or cartoons. Use colour to make these more engaging and memorable.

- Review the entries that you've written over a period of time (e.g. in the past few weeks, or for a study activity, such as completing an assignment). See if you can find key themes from your entries, and recognise what longer term action you might need to take (e.g. to improve a particular study skill).

Remember that writing itself can be used as a learning tool: you don't have to use writing only to communicate what you know and understand (e.g. by producing an assignment or answering questions in an examination), but you can use writing to explore ideas as a way of understanding them.

For many of us, reflection becomes a more meaningful activity if it can be shared, either in a group or with another student. Putting your thoughts and ideas into words and getting a response from someone else, then perhaps listening to their reactions, makes the process more interactive and developmental. This interaction can be face to face, by telephone or email, with another student or friend.

5 Managing your time and space

When it comes to effective learning, it is not just about finding time to study, but about making the best use of that precious time (see Figure 4). To study and learn successfully you need to master three main areas relating to time management.

- Getting organised and finding appropriate places to study.
- Planning and prioritising on an ongoing basis.
- Dealing with distractions.

Figure 4   Managing your time for learning

5.1 Getting organised and finding study places

You need somewhere to study, and somewhere to keep your course materials, files and books. You'll also need access to a computer. It is not always possible to have a room to yourself that is always available.

- You could regularly use the kitchen or dining room table.

- Boxes or bags can be used to store materials you are currently using to say, prepare for an assignment. A bag can even have its own filing system and you can take it wherever you need to go – on the train to work, in the garden if you feel like some fresh air, or to the local library.

It can be good to use a particular study space regularly because when you go and sit there it becomes habitual to start studying. You can use this kind of established space for fairly long periods of study, but you'll also need other study spaces for shorter bursts of activity – it is quite remarkable what you can achieve in only 10-20 minutes, for example.

- Listen to an audio recording in your car to review course material.

- Study in a waiting room before an appointment.

Think ahead about the handy study materials you'll need for these times, such as using index cards of your notes. Once you get in the habit of finding opportunities to study it becomes second nature.

 To find out more about using audio for your studies go to Skills for OU Study at http://www.open.ac.uk/skillsforstudy/.

You'll also need to find the places and times that work best for you. Perhaps your optimum study session is:

- in a quiet area without distraction, or with background noise or music

- in short bursts, or marathon sessions (but remember to take breaks)

- early mornings, daytime or evenings or nights

- using a PC, or making handwritten notes

- walking about, or sitting with snacks and drinks.

Always try to:

- do the most difficult work when your concentration is strongest
- take regular breaks, perhaps every hour
- be flexible – reflect on whether your study pattern is successful. For example, if you are getting less done in the evenings than you hoped, try something different, perhaps by studying in the early morning.

> ❝ I'm really a morning person, but I might think about doing a bit before dinner though if I'm home at a reasonable time. It's worth studying for half an hour or so at a time – over a week it adds up. ❞

Being organised is not necessarily about being tidy – it's about having a system in place that works for you so that it is easy to find things while you're tackling difficult study tasks, and trying to fit study in to your life.

5.2 Planning and prioritising

You need to identify your goals relating to your studies and then plan accordingly.

- Long-term goals. Plan ahead so that you can regularly prioritise short term goals. When are the assignment deadlines for my course? What are my commitments and plans for the year (e.g. when is the family holiday? Do I have key events at work, which will impact on my study time and how I feel about studying?)

- Short-term goals. What shall I do with the study time I've put aside today? What is important today for this week's goals? How am I feeling? Would I be better off if I actively read a section of course material, or worked out the tasks I need to do to complete my assignment?

Long-term goals

A valuable method of planning is to create a schedule that includes all your key commitments relating to your study, your work, and personal or social life. Depending on your course of study or programme, a long-term schedule that covers a few months, or the whole year can be very useful. A wall planner can be effective for this purpose so you get the big picture. You'll then be able to see your course deadlines in the light of other commitments in your life.

You could use your course calendar for this task by adding the other commitments you have. Alternatively, you could refer to the course calendar when you are filling in your wall planner, or drawing up your schedule for the next year.

Make sure you are very familiar with your course.

- What is required to pass the course?
- When are the assignment cut-off dates?
- What are the learning outcomes?
- How much time do you need to allocate to study?

Recommended study time is around 100 hours study for each 10 points of a course. So work out how much study time each week you need to put aside and review this regularly as you go through your studies.

Short-term goals

Think about your short-term goals, such as completing an assignment. You can do this with a more detailed plan or timetable so that you can break down a particular activity into more manageable chunks, which you can tackle in the study sessions you have available. This schedule might be for the next week or few weeks. Put the plan or schedule on the wall, or fridge, or stick it on the front page of your learning journal or note book – and try and keep to it (see Figure 5).

Consider using incentives and rewards, to help you:

- to motivate yourself to get started on a particular study task
- to stick to your study schedule
- to achieve your short-term goals.

What do you really like doing? Promise yourself a relaxing swim, lunch with a friend, or your favourite TV programme if, for example, you

- do at least two hours of study one day
- keep to your schedule
- send your assignment in on time.

It's good to reward yourself to help you stick to your plans, but remember that you may need to revise schedules and timetables from time to time. You shouldn't worry about this as sometimes certain course readings can take longer than you expected – you'll just need to re-plan a bit, and you'll find that with practise you'll get better at estimating how long particular study tasks will take you.

> ❛ I now make sure that whatever I'm working on I give myself a reward after forty-five minutes. It's something to look forward to and it keeps me going. I might only stop for about two or three minutes and other times I take up to fifteen minutes – it depends how I feel. It's made a tremendous difference. ❜

Weekly schedules or timetables can help you to see how much time you have available to study, as you can also write in those times when you'll be working, or spending time with the family, for example. You may need to reorganise how you use your time in order to fit sufficient study hours into your week.

Target	What I need to do	With help from	Target date	Revised date	Date completed
Find out what the next TMA is about	read the question and student advice	Bob – self-help group tutor at tutorial	April 12		April 12
Gather material for both parts of essay	go through my notes extracting relevant bits check back through course unit and margin notes in case there is anything to add.	TV programme might be useful	April 13		April 13
Produce an essay plan for each part	put the points in order	discuss key points with Bob	April 13		April 13
Produce first draft of both parts	put my notes in some sort of order with an introduction and conclusion		April 13	April 14	April 14
Produce final draft of part 1	edit to make sure that all the points are relevant; proof read for spelling and grammar 'blips'	self-help group meeting at pub	April 14	April 15	April 15
Produce final draft of part 2	as above	as above	April 16	April 17	April 17
Meet TMA deadline: April 21	have final read through (just in case!) and post to tutor		April 18	April 19	April 19

Figure 5   Example plan

Use daily or weekly 'to do' lists to help you to plan and prioritise. These can also help to clear your mind and clarify what is really important for your studies, but they can also result in you making a commitment to yourself that you will do what you have planned and listed. It can be satisfying to tick-off the tasks you've completed on a list.

Planning is no guarantee everything will get done or that deadlines will be met, and you'll work out what works best for you, but the process of making a plan helps you focus on what the task entails and gives direction and purpose to your study.

Using action plans

An action plan can help you to identify what you want to achieve in the long term, and think through the steps you need to take in the short term to achieve this. This can make it easier to help you realise your goals. Your action plan could include these elements (see Figure 6).

- Goal
- What?
- How?
- Resources?
- When?

A plan or action plan can be just a list of things to do, a chart giving deadlines, a diagram showing how the various parts of your plan interact, or a set of post-its on a sheet of card that you move around when each task is done. If you break down the overall task into a series of smaller targets, you can chart your progress in more detail. It's useful to have a way of recording your progress as well as a way of listing any sources of help that you need.

 Go to http://www.open.ac.uk/skillsforstudy/ to find out more about managing your time effectively.

5.3 Distractions and procrastination

Sometimes it can be difficult to make a start on your studies because you might have distractions to deal with, and you may find that you put off a study task. Distractions can be very real (e.g. your child needs your attention), but they can also be displacement or replacement activities, or ways of procrastinating in disguise.

Instead of getting on with the reading for your assignment you find that all of a sudden you really need to sort out the garden shed, or spring-clean a cupboard. We all experience this from time to time, but it is worth getting to know what kind of displacement activities you tend to engage in – you'll learn to recognise them and deal with them so that you can get down to your important study tasks.

	Action plan
My goal	a degree within four years
What?	need to do 60 points per year
	allocate realistic time for study (i.e. 12 hours per week)
How?	do breakdown of typical week
	note best and worst times of day for study
	timetable in 12 hours using as much 'best time' as possible. Think about which study tasks I might tackle during 'difficult' times, e.g. watching course videos
Resources?	Tom, my line manager - negotiate some study leave and/or flexible working hours
	Clare - to add key family commitments to timetable (eg parents' evenings)
	parents – ask for help with children and garden
When?	talk to Tom during my appraisal on 10 November
	talk to Clare next weekend while children are at swimming lessons and do timetable
	ask Mum and Dad over for a meal next week

Figure 6   Example action plan

Deal with distractions by:

- setting realistic goals for your study session (e.g. 'I'll read this section, or work for 40 minutes before I make that coffee')

- aiming to minimise real interruptions (e.g. putting on your answer phone, politely asking friends not to disturb you).

Working under pressure

Some people say that they need the pressure of a deadline to get on with a (now urgent) study task, such as finally writing an assignment. If you do this, ask yourself whether this way of working is really effective – you could be putting yourself under unnecessary pressure. And although you might feel that you are producing good-quality work under such pressure, you might produce even better work under less stress.

Try to recognise how you might be getting side tracked, or putting things off. Sometimes, these activities do relate to your studies. For example, you may not feel ready to start writing your assignment because you think you need to spend more time reading or taking notes. Remember that it is best to try and have short-term deadlines that you stick to for significant study activities, such as completing an assignment by the cut-off date. You need to find ways to ensure that you can meet deadlines.

- You could ask others for help – what could you delegate?

- Try not to feel that you need to produce the perfect assignment or project.

- Avoid taking on too many commitments – learn to politely say 'no'.

- Learn to prioritise your tasks.

- Do a deal with yourself – 'Okay, I'll go to the pub with my friend who's just phoned, but this means that I'll need to get up early on Sunday to study instead'.

- Just do it! You may find that the task doesn't take as long as you expected and you'll feel much better for getting it out of the way.

In other words, it is worth looking to see if you (unintentionally) put important things off by engaging in other activities. This behaviour is natural, but it can be beneficial to recognise your own patterns so that you can prioritise and get down to your study tasks.

6 In conclusion

As a student you'll develop study strategies that suit you, and learn to recognise which study skills and techniques are valuable for particular tasks and challenges. You'll also find that reflecting on what works well in your studies will help you to develop as you try out different approaches and review their effectiveness.

During your studies, you'll harness a range of existing skills (e.g. organisational and planning skills) and acquire new skills, which will be invaluable in other areas of your life (e.g. in paid or voluntary work). These will include transferable or what are often know as employability skills, such as initiative, problem solving and computer literacy.

Knowing when you need help and where to go for it is important especially if you discover that you need to improve particular study skills. Sources of help may be your tutor or study adviser, or your regional centre.

Remember that you don't always have to study on your own, as you can keep in touch with other students to share ideas, techniques and tips. To do this you can set up or join a study group, or use the OU chat forums online. Many courses run online forums where you can also take part in discussions.

References

Cottrell, S. (2003) Skills for Success. The Personal Development Planning Handbook. Palgrave Macmillan. New York.